A DORYFUL OF NEWFOUNDLAND
LAUGHS

National Library of Canada Cataloguing in Publication

Duggan, Derm
A doryful of Newfoundland laughs / by Derm Duggan. -- 2nd ed.

ISBN 978-1-897317-47-1

1. Canadian wit and humor (English)--Newfoundland and Labrador. 2. Newfoundland and Labrador--Humor. I. Title.

PN6178.C3D875 2009 C818'.602 C2009-902318-0

MIX Paper from responsible sources FSC® C016245 FSC www.fsc.org

This paper has been certified to meet the environmental and social standards of the Forest Stewardship Council® (FSC®) and comes from responsibly managed forests, and verified recycled sources.

PRINTED IN CANADA

FLANKER PRESS
PO BOX 2522, STATION C
ST. JOHN'S, NL, CANADA
TOLL FREE: 1-866-739-4420
WWW.FLANKERPRESS.COM

9 8 7 6 5 4 3

Canada | Canada Council for the Arts | Conseil des Arts du Canada | Newfoundland Labrador

We acknowledge the [financial] support of the Government of Canada. *Nous reconnaissons l'appui [financier] du gouvernement du Canada.* We acknowledge the support of the Canada Council for the Arts, which last year invested $153 million to bring the arts to Canadians throughout the country. *Nous remercions le Conseil des arts du Canada de son soutien. L'an dernier, le Conseil a investi 153 millions de dollars pour mettre de l'art dans la vie des Canadiennes et des Canadiens de tout le pays.* We acknowledge the financial support of the Government of Newfoundland and Labrador, Department of Tourism, Culture and Recreation for our publishing activities.

A DORYFUL OF NEWFOUNDLAND
LAUGHS

SECOND EDITION

BY DERM DUGGAN

Flanker Press Ltd.
St. John's
2009

"Doctor, Doctor, quick. I need help."

"What's your problem?"

"Doctor, I can't sleep, I can't work, I can't eat. You see, I think I am a bird."

After an hour's discussion with the patient, the doctor instructed his patient. "You can go now. Remember what I tell you. It's all in your mind."

"Thank you, Doctor, I feel relieved."

The patient opened the window and flew out.

Speaking of weather forecasts, there was the viewer who phoned the Wal-Mart Service Department in the Avalon Mall.

Viewer: "I'm looking at the TV right now. Debbie Cooper is on and she has a long face."

Serviceman: "So would you, ma'am, if you had to report the news these days!"

Rookie reporter at NTV to veteran:

Rookie: "I've been assigned to the House of Assembly. How will I know if an MHA is lying when I do an interview?"

Vet: "Simple, son. If he strokes his hair, he's telling the truth. If he scratches his nose, he's also telling the truth. If he tugs his ear, he's still telling the truth ... but if he moves his lips, he's lying!"

"DO YOU REALIZE THAT THERE ARE SIXTY-FOUR EMPTY BOTTLES IN OUR BASEMENT?"

"THASH STRANGE, I DONT REMEMBER EVER BRINGING HOME ANY EMPTY BOTTLES"

Man: "Get ready to die. I'm going to shoot you."
Victim: "Why?"
Man: "I've always said I'd shoot anyone who looked like me."
Victim: "Do I look like you?"
Man: "Yes."
Victim: "Then shoot!"

The wily old MHA was being sued. He told the lawyer to appear in court for him, and also instructed the lawyer to send the verdict by fax to his constituency office.

When the verdict was handed down, the lawyer sent the following message, "Justice has prevailed."

The MHA faxed him back, "Appeal at once."

A bayman and a townie were fishing on opposite sides of the same pond.

In the evening, they met at the roadwise where their cars were parked.

The bayman had a dozen pan-sized trout on his creel. The townie was staggering under the weight of a single huge fish, the biggest ever caught in that pond. It was about five feet long and must have weighed eighty pounds.

The townie said, "Hey! Look what I got!"

Said the bayman, with a shrug, "Only caught the one, eh?"

"KNOW WHAT? I'VE GOT ME SELF A WHITE HEN THAT KIN LAY BLACK EGGS"
"WELL, I CAN'T SEE WHAT'S SO WONDERFUL ABOUT THAT"
"KIN YOU DO IT?"
DERM DUGGAN ©

The priest addressed the churchgoers. "As you all know, the husband of a widow in our parish has been dead for one year. Now there is one person here in this congregation who goes to her house every evening to spend the night there. I know who this person is, and if I don't see a ten-dollar bill in the collection plate this morning, I'm going to write his name on this blackboard so everyone can see."

When the collection was taken there were thirty-two tens and one five-dollar bill with a note attached. It read, "Please don't write my name on the blackboard, Father. I'll give you the other five next week."

Overheard at the Avalon Mall:

"I swear I don't know what to make of the younger generation," said one patron. "Spiky hair, dyed all colours, green, orange and purple; tight leather pants or extra-short shorts; t-shirts with the indecent messages printed on 'em; massive earrings; and those powerful colognes."

"Yeah! said his companion, shaking his head, "and the women are worse!"

Man: "This is my travelling suit."

Friend: "Travelling suit?"

Man: "Yeah, it travelled from my father down to me."

Two hunters, Pat and Mike, were returning home from a long day in the woods when their car broke down on a lonely country road. Fortunately, they saw a light in a farmhouse just across the road.

They went up and knocked on the door and explained their plight to the gorgeous widow who answered. She invited them in, fed them a sumptuous meal, and put them up for the night.

In the morning, she took her new Cadillac out of the barn and drove them to the nearest town, where they arranged to have their car towed in and repaired.

Three months later, Pat got a phone call from Mike.

"Pat," said Mike, "did you sleep with that gorgeous widow that night?"

"Yes, Mike," said Pat, "I have to admit I did."

"And did you give her my name and address instead of your own?"

"I have to admit, Mike that I did. Why, what's wrong?"

"Oh, nothing," replied Mike. "You see, she just died and left me the farmhouse, five hundred acres of land and that new Cadillac in the barn."

On his way into the Cotton Club on George Street, the young Newfoundland trawlerman was accosted by a street preacher.

"If you go into that den of iniquity, young man," warned the evangelist, "the devil goes with you."

"Well, if he does, buddy," replied the sailor, "he'll pay his own way. Nobody freeloads on me!"

Jack, a boarding student at M.U.N., came into the room looking mournful, clutching a letter.

Fred, his roommate, asked, "What's the matter, Jack? You look down in the dumps."

"I said I was cold and wrote home for money for a blanket."

"So what?"

"They're sending the blanket!"

Overheard at the Stone House restaurant:

First diner: "You know, my wife made a millionaire out of me."

Second diner: "Really? And what were you before?"

First diner: "A multi-millionaire."

A man brushed past the receptionist and rushed into the doctor's office. He had a wild look on his face.

"Doc," he said breathlessly, "sorry to barge in like this, but it's been a whole week with no letup and no relief. Do you know any way to stop the hiccups?"

The doctor got up, stepped around the desk, and slapped him across the face.

"Why did you do that?" asked the man.

"Well," said the doctor, smiling, "you don't have the hiccups now, do you?"

"No," said the man, "but my wife outside still does!"!"

The salesman at Cohen's was showing the yuppie couple a big colour television set.

"You make a small down payment," said the salesman, "and then you pay nothing for a whole year."

"Who's been in here backbiting us?" demanded the yuppies.

During a medical convention at the Delta Hotel in downtown St. John's, an elderly psychiatrist was being interviewed by a young reporter from VOCM.

"How long have you been practicing psychiatry in Newfoundland, doctor?" asked the reporter.

"I began my practice in Corner Brook forty years ago," replied the psychiatrist, "and I still have a full schedule of patients with problems six days a week, sometimes seven."

"That's remarkable," said the reporter, "and it's even more remarkable that you can listen to patients' problems for a lifetime and not feel depressed."

"Who listens?"

Overheard in a Toronto bar:

First drinker: "I hear those Newfies are the toughest fighters in the world. They can lick anyone."

Second drinker: "Aw, they're not so tough. Jack, Tom, Bill, Pete and I beat one up just the other day."

Overheard at the Delta Hotel bar:

First young lady: "My new lover is rich, he's generous, he has a great pad at the Tiffany, and he drives a completely original 1929 Packard Roadster."

Second young lady: "Fantastic!"

First young lady: "Yeah! But he's also the original owner."

They strolled down the lane together
The sky was brilliant with stars
They reached the gate in silence,
He lifted for her the bars.
She neither smiled nor thanked him,
Because she knew not how;
For he was just a farmer's boy
And she was a Jersey cow.

The two Newfoundland fisherman at Bauline were talking about the local weatherman and his often inaccurate weather forecasts.

Said one fisherman, "Better not complain, b'y. 'Tis bad enough he's only predictin' the weather. How bad would it be if he was regulatin' it?"

"SO THINGS ARE BAD, LOOK 'OL MAN WHY DON'T YOU DROWN YOUR TROUBLES?"

"LISHEN BUDDY, I WOULD GLADLY, BUT I CAN'T GET 'ER TO GO SWIMMING WIT ME"

On his popular evening talk show, the host had to cope with this one:

Caller: "Good evening, sir."

Host: "And how are you this grand evening, m'lovely?"

Caller: "Oh, sir! I hope you can help me. I just read where all the churches are removing the word 'obey' from the marriage service."

Host: "Yes, m'lovely. I read that too."

Caller: "Can you tell me if it's retroactive?"

On a motor trip through New England, the Newfoundland tycoon stopped in a little New Hampshire town for a bite to eat.

"I'll have a western sandwich and a cup of coffee," the tycoon ordered.

"Sorry, sir," said the pretty waitress, "I can't give you a western."

The big wheel was annoyed. "Why not?" he growled.

"Around here," said the waitress with a dimpled smile, "we only serve easterns!"

The homely looking woman says to the psychiatrist, "My problem is, Doctor, that I feel I'm so ugly no man would want to look at me."

Says the psychiatrist, "Let's talk about it. Just go over there and lie face down on the couch."

George, from Heart's Content, was staying at the Inn-on-the-Park in Toronto.

In the bar, George struck up a conversation with a tourist from Texas.

"Where are you from?" asked George.

"I'm from the greatest place in the whole wide world," drawled the Texan.

"You sure could've fooled me," said George. "You don't sound a bit like a Newfoundlander!"

The ad man went to see his psychiatrist.

"Doc," he said, "I'm worried. I've never lost an account. I don't wear three-button suits with vests, or boned wing-tip shoes. I don't wear oxford shirts with button-down collars, or sincere silk ties. I don't drink and I never tell lies."

"Then what's the trouble?" asked the psychiatrist.

"Tell me Doc – am I normal?"

The old Newfoundland fisherman was sitting on the pier puffing on his pipe.

The young NTV reporter doing street interviews approached him and asked: "Sir, what do you think of the prediction that in the year 2000 women will rule the world?"

"Still, eh?"

Driving across from St. Stephen to Calais, the two Newfoundland travellers stopped at a small store in Maine.

The store had a prominent sign stating: "We accept Canadian money at par."

At the checkout, one traveller made a rapid mental calculation and put down a Canadian ten-dollar bill and a loonie.

The cashier, unfamiliar with the coin, picked it up and stared at it curiously.

The other traveller told her, "That's a loonie."

"I don't care if he's a talking baboon," said the cashier, "just as long as his money's good!"

Speaking of miniskirts, they really bring out the courteous qualities in the men of this province.

You'll never see a Newfoundlander get on an escalator ahead of one.

Effie and Archie were in church one evening when the lights went out.

Later, when the lights came on again, Effie said: "Archie, you shouldn't have kissed me like that with all those people around, even if it was dark."

"I didn't kiss you," said Archie. "If I knew who did, I'd teach him a thing or two."

"Archie," sighed Effie, "you couldn't teach him a thing!"

Remember when you were small? You'd tell your mother you'd be good for five cents. Now that you're all grown up you're good for nothing.

Remember, don't smoke. The ashes that fall on the floor may be your own.

> The reason the colour of the elephant is grey is so that you won't get it mixed up with a blueberry.

The boss said you should have been here at 8:30.
Why, what happened?

Is this the office of the War on Poverty Committee?
It is.
Okay. I came here to surrender.

For the fifth time in three weeks, a mother took her young son to see the psychiatrist at the medical clinic.

Once more, Dr. O'Brien examined the boy, and once more found nothing wrong.

"Your son is just fine," he told the mother, "he's a normal healthy boy. It's you I'm concerned about. You're fretting too much about your son. I'm prescribing tranquilizers for you. Take three of these every day and come back to see me in a month."

A month later, the mother came back alone to see the doctor.

"How's your son?" asked Dr. O'Brien.

"Who cares?"

Man: "I wish I were like the rivers."

Friend: "What for?"

Man: "To follow my course without leaving my bed."

The Newfoundland insurance man was just entering the restaurant when a friend hailed him from a nearby table.

When the waitress arrived, the insurance man said he'd just have coffee.

"Are you on a diet?" asked his friend.

"No," was the answer, "on commission!"

Skipper walked into a bar and ordered two big drinks. He drank one and poured the other one in his pocket. Then he ordered two more and did the same thing again.

The bartender spoke up. "Listen here, pal. You can drink all you want, but I hate to see you pour one in your pocket each time."

Skipper up and said, "Mind your own business or I'll jump over this bar and break your neck."

Suddenly, a drunken mouse sticks his head out of the man's pocket and says, "And that goes for your cat, too!"

"I was in a little accident and it was all a case of mistaken identity," said one man to his friend.

"A case of mistaken identity? Tell me about it."

"Well," the man said, "I took my girlfriend out to dinner last night and we goes into a small restaurant. We walks in and orders a big meal, and no sooner started to eat than my girl found a bug in her soup!"

His friend said, "That was terrible. What did she do?"

"She yelled, 'Waiter remove this insect!'"

"Well?"

"He threw me down two flights of stairs."

Sign in Sex Research Bureau: "Please feel free to indulge in a little foreplay while you wait."

The noted Newfoundland artist was showing a friend around his studio. All over the place were dozens of huge canvases with abstract designs in swirls of wild colours.

"These are unusual," said the friend. "How do you do them?"

"I put the canvas on the floor, take pots of paint, all different colours, and spill paint on the canvas. Then I get a couple of nude models to slither all over it. I call them my little brushes."

"Interesting," remarked the friend. "Evidently, you sell a lot of them."

"Matter of fact, I can't sell 'em at all," said the artist, "but I sure have fun cleaning the brushes."

Bill: "What are you doing, Ron, snapping your fingers together?"

Ron: "I'm keeping the elephants away."

"Bill: "Are you crazy? There are no elephants within miles of here. The nearest elephant is in Africa."

Ron: "It's working, ain't it?"

They say the world is getting smaller.

Then why is Canada Post raising the price of stamps again?

Two women were discussing marriage and the conversation went like this.

"Well, how many times were you married?"

"Three times."

"What? Three times? Are any of your husbands living?"

"No. All dead."

"What happened to your first husband?"

"He died of mushroom poisoning."

"And your second husband?"

"Same thing, mushroom poisoning."

"And what happened to your third husband?"

"He died of a heavy blow to the head."

"What happened?"

"He wouldn't eat his mushrooms."

A drunk phoned the owner of a club and said, "What time does your club open?"

The owner said, "It closes 2:30 and it doesn't open until 10:00 in the morning."

An hour later the drunk called again. This time the owner, annoyed, said, "I told you. We open at 10:00. Now hang up and leave me alone."

At 4:00 in the morning the drunk called again. Fed up, the owner said, "You know what I told you before. You must be some desperate to get in."

"No sir," the drunk said, "I'm trying to get out."

The Newfoundland political figure was hitting the campaign trail from dawn to dusk in his effort to unseat Clyde Wells.

When he and his wife got home one evening, the wife flaked out on the sofa, saying, "Either send out for Chinese or get a meal yourself – I'm too tired to cook."

"You're tired!" exclaimed the politician. "What about me? I made fourteen speeches today."

"You mean," replied his spouse wearily, "you made the same speech fourteen times, and I had to listen to all of it. I'm not just tired, I'm mesmerized!"

The Newfoundland political gadfly took his wife to England on a holiday.

They were at the bar in the Peacock and Rose pub, discussing their travels. A stranger sitting next to them interrupted, saying, "Pardon me, but I couldn't help overhearing you. Would you tell me where you're from? You have such a distinctive accent."

The pair looked at him coldly. Then, ignoring the stranger, the husband spoke to his wife. "Mixed up, ain't he? He's the one with the accent!"

Overheard at the Pearly Gates:
St. Peter: "Who's knocking?"
Cultured voice: "It is I."
St. Peter: "Good Lord! Another schoolteacher!"

An eccentric old Newfoundland prospector struck gold over in St. George's Bay, but died on the way in to Corner Brook to register his claim.

On his deathbed, he drew a map to the treasure, then tore it in two. In his will, he left half the map to each of his friends, Harley and Jock, on the unusual condition that each put a thousand dollars in his coffin.

Harley, an American, put in his thousand.

Jock, a Scotsman, removed Harley's cash, and put in a cheque for two thousand, payable to the bearer. That same day, the old prospector was buried.

When Jock got his bank statement the first of the month, he was astonished to see that his cheque had been cashed. It had been endorsed by Pat, the undertaker, a Newfoundlander.

One day, Sam didn't get up to go to work. He stayed in bed all day, saying he was sick.

Sam's wife called the doctor, who came and examined him thoroughly.

"I can't find anything wrong with him," said the doctor. "He only thinks he's sick."

The very next day Sam's wife called the doctor again.

"You'd better come quick, Doc," she blurted. "Now he thinks he's dead!"

In his capacity as federal Minister of Fisheries, John Crosbie summoned a pair of prominent union chiefs, along with a Fisheries Department mandarin, to a meeting in his office. He wanted to discuss the crisis in the Newfoundland fishery.

Just as the meeting got underway, a courier arrived with a package for Crosbie. In the package was a corked bottle. A constituent had found it on the beach in St. Mary's Bay and sent it to Crosbie unopened as a gift.

Crosbie set the bottle aside to resume the meeting, but the other three insisted that he open the bottle and see what was in it.

When Crosbie pulled out the cork, a genie appeared.

"Four hundred years ago," said the genie, "an evil witch cast a spell over me and imprisoned me in that bottle. I've been there ever since. Now, thanks to you gentlemen, I'm free at last. So, to show my gratitude, I'll grant each of you one wish."

The first union leader piped up promptly: "I want to go to a beautiful tropic isle, where I'll be fabulously rich, and have my every need and whim attended to by a score of gorgeous women."

"Granted immediately," said the genie, and the first union leader vanished in a swirl of wind and a puff of smoke.

Then the second union leader spoke up: "I want to be king of a wonderful country, where I'll be fabulously rich, and where my adoring subjects will attend to my every need and whim."

"Granted immediately," said the genie, and the second union leader vanished in a swirl of wind and a puff of smoke.

The federal Fisheries mandarin was next. He told the genie: "My father was a fisherman, and I've always loved the sea. I want to go live aboard the world's most luxurious yacht, where I'll be fabulously rich, and where my lovely female crew will cater to my every need and whim."

"Granted immediately," said the genie, and the mandarin also vanished in a swirl of wind and a puff of smoke.

The genie turned to John Crosbie. "Now, sir," he said, "what is your wish?"

"That's easy," replied Crosbie. "I want those three back here pronto!"

"I WONDER IF MY GIRL LOVES ME?"
"Y' KNOW SHE DOES"
"WHY WOULD SHE MAKE YOU AN EXCEPTION?"
DERM DUGGAN ©

During the armed confrontation at Oka, Quebec, Joe Clark was sent in to try and settle the dispute.

In a clearing in the woods behind the barricades, Clark addressed a large group of Mohawk warriors.

"The federal government is aware of your concerns, and will act to help you."

"Um-bagah! Um-bagah!" shouted the warriors.

"If you will lay down your arms, and give yourselves up, you will not be charged with any offenses."

"Um-bagah! Um-bagah!" chanted the warriors, laughing and waving their arms.

Encouraged, Clark continued, "We will sit down with your leaders at the conference table and negotiate as equals."

More laughter from the warriors, with much waving of arms, and pointing at Clark. "Um-bagah!" they roared. "Um-bagah!"

Said Clark to one of the chiefs, "I believe they have confidence in me to deal fairly. This is going well; but I must take a moment to answer a call of nature. Where shall I go?"

"Just follow that moose track into the woods over there," replied the chief, pointing.

"Thank you, sir," said clark.

"One more thing, Mr. Clark," said the chief. "When you go in there, be careful not to step in the um-bagah."

Remember when ... Safe sex used to be when the husband worked the night shift.

Father Jim Doody, the parish priest at St. Mary's, phones the town council and reported that a jackass had dropped dead right in front of the church.

"Could you have the carcass removed, please?" asked Father Jim.

"I thought you priests took care of the dead," said the town clerk slyly.

"We do! We do!" said Father Jim. "But first we have to notify their relatives."

The Newfoundland economy is so bad that some of our biggest businessmen are even taking politicians off the payroll.

This big bully at the old Belmont Tavern on New Gower Street was mean and ugly. At once boastful, loud and threatening, he was spoiling for a fight.

A mild-looking old trawlerman came in and took a barstool near the bully. Waiting for his beer, he glanced idly around, and caught the bully's eye.

"Who d'ya think yer lookin' at, old man?" snarled the bully, truculently.

The trawlerman's beer was in front of him by now. He took a thoughtful sip, then looked the bully in the eye.

"Well, now," said the old trawlerman, "since ye want to know, I'll tell ye. Thirty-some years ago, I interfered with a pig and I was thinkin' that ye just might be my son."

A multi-millionaire Newfoundland businessman got a tip that he could pick up the Harbour Castle Inn in Toronto for a mere 20 million dollars.

He summoned a trusted aide and told him to go buy it. "Don't go over 20 million for it," he cautioned.

The aide came back a couple of days later and said, "Boss, I've got good news and bad news."

"What's the good news?" asked the boss.

"We can snap it up for just 18 million," the aide told him.

"Then what's the bad news?"

"They want two thousand dollars down – in cash!"

The day that Newfoundland Citizenship Judge Tom Osborne administered the oath of allegiance, the Hindu couple was ecstatic.

Arriving home, Madhu gave his wife an exuberant hug.

"Ah, Surekha!" he exclaimed, "how fortunate we are! Now you can write all our friends back in Bombay, and tell them you've become a real Newfoundland housewife."

"Yes! It's wonderful. And it changes everything," said Surekha, handing him her apron. "From now on, Madhu, you'll be doing the dishes!"

"SON, I WANT YOU TO KNOW THAT THE ONLY REASON I SPANKED YOU IS.... BECAUSE I LOVE YOU"
"YEAH, WELL I WISH I WAS BIG ENOUGH TO RETURN YOUR LOVE!"
DERM DUGGAN ©

The big eighteen-wheeler pulled in at the roadside diner, and the small, slender driver went in and ordered soup with steak and fries.

He had just started to eat, when three burly bikers swaggered in.

As they passed the trucker's table, the first biker took his steak; the second biker took his plate of fries; and the third biker pushed his face in his soup.

The trucker got up, wiped his face in his napkin, dropped a bill on the table, and walked out.

"Cluck! Cluck!" said the first biker, "there goes a chicken."

"Yeah, but not a peep out of him," sneered the second biker.

"I guess that's one chicken that laid an egg," laughed the third biker. "That's one chicken that can't fight."

"Can't drive either," said the waitress, looking out the window. "He just ran over three bikes!"

Clyde Wells, the premier of Newfoundland, and John Crosbie, the federal Minister of fisheries, were talking about Brian Mulroney, the Prime Minister of Canada, and his low rating in the polls.

"Poor Brian," said Crosbie, "you have to feel sorry for him. He's brought this on himself, you know. He's his own worst enemy."

"Not while I'm alive," said Clyde.

There was this parrot in Ottawa that escaped from a house of ill repute.

The bird was caught downtown by a meter maid, who sold it to a pet shop.

The prime minister's wife spotted the parrot in the pet shop and brought it home for the kids.

Soon after, the prime minister and his wife threw a dinner party for all his cabinet ministers and their wives.

When the guests assembled in the drawing room after dinner, the prime minister's wife decided to take the hood off the parrot's cage.

The parrot looked around the room with interest.

"Nice new room!" he squawked.

Then he looked at the ladies.

"All new women!" he cackled.

Finally, he sized up the men.

"Same old customers!"

Overheard at Bally Haly:

"I see where some Russian has invented a game that closely resembles golf."

"I know that game. My friend Barry has been playing it for years!"

Overheard at the Goulds race track:

"Strange that our friend Martin has such bad luck betting on the horses – especially when he's so lucky at cards."

"Nothing strange about that. He can't shuffle the horse."

The latest member of Brian Mulroney's cabinet to resign called in his successor. He gave the new minister three sealed envelopes.

"The very first time anything goes wrong," the outgoing minister told the new man, "open the first envelope right away. The next time there's a problem, open the second envelope. Keep the third envelope till last."

A week later, the new minister was being severely criticized in the press, so he opened the first envelope. Inside was a note that read, "Blame it on your predecessor." He did so and the storm blew over.

Three months later the new minister faced another big criticism, so he opened the second envelope. The note inside read, "Reorganize the department." He did so and the storm blew over.

A year later, things started going wrong again, and the situation began to look pretty desperate. So the minister opened the third envelope.

The message inside began, "Prepare three envelopes ..."

New bride: "The two best things I cook are fish and brewis, and Jiggs Dinner."

New groom: "Which one is this, dearest?"

George: "I won $50,000."

Gerald: "Fifty thousand? Clear?"

George: "No, I had to pay two dollars for the ticket."

"I WAS WONDERING WHAT YOU WOULD SAY IF I ASKED YOU TO BECOME MY WIFE?"
"NOT MUCH I CAN'T TALK AND LAUGH AT THE SAME TIME"
DERMOT DUGGAN ©

Young man to priest:

"Tell me, Father, why did God make some women so beautiful?"

"So you'd be attracted to them, my son."

"But, Father, why did he make some of the beautiful ones so dumb?"

"So they'd be attracted to you, my son."

Two hunters in an open field, in the ominous black shadow of an enormous bird.

One hunter says: "You and your goddam duck calls!"

Newfoundland's eighth Lieutenant-Governor, Jim McGrath, was elected to the House of Commons when he was only 25 years old. Up to that time, he was the youngest member ever elected to Canada's Parliament.

When the announcement of his candidacy appeared in The Evening Telegram, a friend of his mother's remarked to her husband: "I see young McGrath's thrown his diaper into the ring!"

"DO YOU MIND IF I TRY ON THAT DRESS IN THE WINDOW?"
"WHY NOT... IT MIGHT BE GOOD FOR BUSINESS!"
DERM DUGGAN ©

Former premier Brian Peckford tells the one about the 88-year-old widower in his Green Bay riding who took a vacation trip to Banff.

When he got back, he called on his relatives to come over and meet his new bride.

"You got married!" they exclaimed incredulously. "Who is she?"

"This here's Diane," he told them proudly, "and she turned eighteen last week."

"But Grampa," gasped one of the clan, "how could you think of marrying such a young girl?"

"She's not so young," replied the oldster. "Your grandma was only fifteen when I married her."

Then there was the grizzled old fisherman in Joe Batt's Arm who was invited to the S.U.F. Hall to meet Brian Mulroney.

"Who's Brian Mulroney?" he wanted to know.

"Do you mean to say you never heard of Brian Mulroney? He's on the radio and television just about every day."

"Well, get to the point. What's he in?" queried the old fellow crossly. "Longliners or trawlers?"

"How far to Deer Lake?" asked the tourist of the strawberry farmer in Pasadena.

"The way you're headed," said the farmer, "it's 940 miles. If you turn the car around, it's ten miles."

"I COMES FROM A TOUGH FAMILY, ME BRUDDER WAS SO HARD HE FACED UP TO MIKE TYSON AND SMACKED 'IM RIGHT IN TH' MOUTH
"ME BOY, I'D LIKE TO MEET HIM - I'D LIKE TO SHAKE HIS HAND"
"YOU DON'T THINK WE'RE GOING TO DIG 'IM UP JUST SO HE KIN SHAKE HANDS WIT YOU"
DERM DUGGAN ©

Standing at the bar, the little drunk stuck out his chin and said to the big drunk, "I'll give you just ten seconds to apologize for those remarks."

"Oh yeah?" said the big drunk with a snarl. "Suppose I won't do it?"

"Well," said the little drunk, "how much time do you need?"

Mike: "After tomorrow, I'm not going to wear these pants any longer."

Johnnie: "Why?"

Mike: "Because they're long enough."

The elderly chap said to the young lady, "I have two million dollars and I'm 85 years old. Will you marry me or am I too old for you?"

The young woman smiled and said, "You have two million dollars and you're 85 years old? Of course I'll marry you! Why, I'd be satisfied if you were ten years older."

Man: "How did you like our jokes?"

Woman: "I can't see anything funny in them."

Man: "Oh, well, you'll probably catch on after a while and laugh."

Woman: "No, I laughed at 'em twenty years ago."

FROM THE PAGES OF . . .

Wife to drunken husband: "So you finally decided to come back. Well, that goes to show you there's no place like home!"

Husband: "It'sh th' only place open."

The hefty woman at the bar was leaning well over – looking miserable.

"Bartender," said she, "I feel lousy. How about some Alka-Seltzer for me heartburn?"

The bartender said, "Lady, you don't need no Alka-Seltzer. Just straighten up – you got your boobs in the ashtray."

Bob and me ain't speaking no more. We wuz gabbing on the street when all of a sudden he punches me in the mouth. What he was telling me was that he makes love to his wife at least three times a day – and all I said was that I knew six guys who did also. Then for no reason that I knows, he flips out and goes ape.

Bob: "I want to apologize for my appearance this evening. This was rather unexpected and I didn't have an opportunity to dress. You know I like to dress for the occasion. Sometimes I change my clothes four or five times a day – if the occasion demands."

Pete: "Bragging, huh? Well, that's nothing. I've got a brother who changes his clothes five times an hour if the occasion demands."

Bob: "How old is he?"

Pete: "Six months."

Skipper phoned the police station and said, "Send someone over quick. My steering wheel is gone. So is my gas pedal, my brake, and even the dash."

Ten minutes later the same man called again. "Disregard my call. I got in the back seat by mistake."

Hank: "I intends to get married soon's I find someone who's me complete opposite."

Will: "OK. I'll look around and see if I can find a beautiful ... cultural ... intelligent ... good girl."

JAKE - IS IT TRUE DID YOU REALLY WIN THE MILLION?
YEP S'TRUE COURSE I DON'T INTEND TO TAKE IT
IN THE NAME OF HEAVEN WHY NOT?
BECAUSE THERE'S NO WAY I'M GOING TO SCREW UP ME UNEMPLOY-MENT INSURANCE

"Hello, doctor! I know it's 3:00 A.M. and I hate to call you at this hour, but my two dogs are joined together and I've tried everything to get them apart. I've even thrown buckets of cold water over them, but nothing worked. Tell me please, tell me what to do!"

The much annoyed doctor said, "Why don't you tell them that they're wanted on the phone?"

"Oh doctor," cried the woman. "Will that stop them?"

"Well ma'am, I can't see why not. It damn well stopped me!"

Two brothers went to Toronto to get jobs. They went to a factory for an interview.

Interviewer: "What can you fellows do?"

First brother: "I makes panty hose."

Second brother: "I'm a diesel fitter."

Interviewer: "Well, a diesel fitter would be useful, but I don't have a job for a panty hose maker. Describe what you do."

Second brother: "Well b'y, me brudder dere makes the panty hose and I holds 'em up and says,"Deese'll fit 'er."

REMEMBER WHEN..

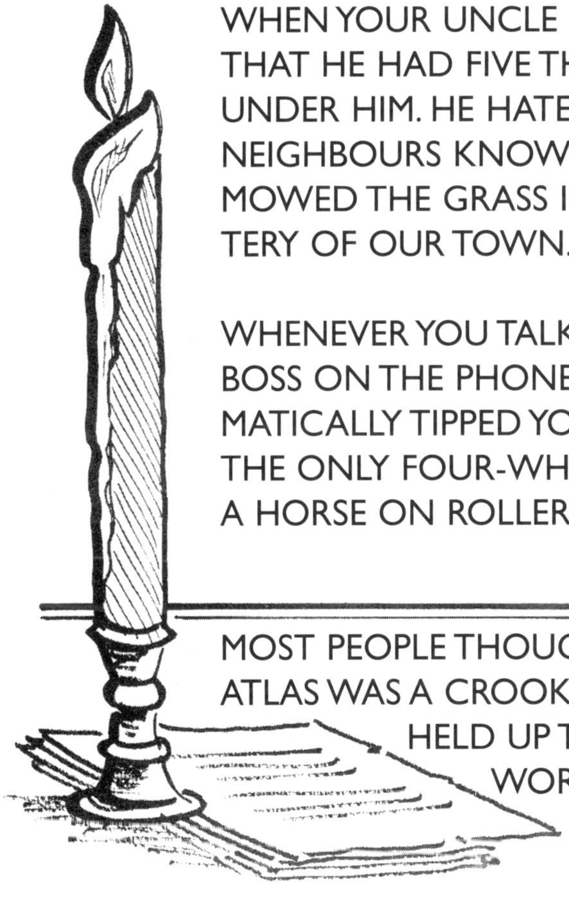

WHEN YOUR UNCLE USED TO BRAG THAT HE HAD FIVE THOUSAND MEN UNDER HIM. HE HATED TO LET THE NEIGHBOURS KNOW THAT HE MOWED THE GRASS IN THE CEMETERY OF OUR TOWN.

WHENEVER YOU TALKED TO THE BOSS ON THE PHONE YOU AUTOMATICALLY TIPPED YOUR HAT – AND THE ONLY FOUR-WHEEL DRIVE WAS A HORSE ON ROLLER SKATES.

MOST PEOPLE THOUGHT CHARLES ATLAS WAS A CROOK BECAUSE HE HELD UP THE WHOLE WORLD.

YOU KNOW SOMETHING I RARELY TELL ANYONE THIS - BUT I HAVE TWO FAULTS - THE FIRST IS DRINKING HARD LIQUOR AND...
WELL SIR AS LONG AS NO ONE KNOWS I CAN TELL YOU MY ONLY WEAKNESS IS I'M HAVING AN AFFAIR WITH WIDOW WHITE
MY OTHER REAL FAULT IS THAT I LOVE TO GOSSIP - FOR THAT REASON I CAN HARDLY WAIT TO TELL THE CONGREGATION ABOUT YOU TWO ON SUNDAY (HEH-HEH)

SIGNS WITH SENSE

DUMBBELL LETTERS

DOCTOR,
EVERY NIGHT I HAVE ALL KINDS OF TROUBLE WITH MY BREATHING. PLEASE GIVE ME SOMETHING THAT WILL STOP THAT.

SINCERELY,
HARRY

DOCTOR,
ME RIGHT LEG IS DRIVING ME CRAZY WITH THE PAIN. WHY DO YOU TELL ME THERE'S NO CURE—THAT IT'S THE RESULT OF OLD AGE?
THERE'S SOMETHING FISHY ABOUT YOU BECAUSE ME LEFT LEG DOESN'T HURT AT ALL—AND THAT'S AS OLD AS ME RIGHT ONE.

SUSPICIOUS

DEAR UNCLE SPIKE,
YOU HAD NO RIGHT TO GIVE MUDDER A BLACK EYE (WHEN THEY LET YOU OUT OF JAIL ON YOUR BIRTHDAY).
SHE JUST DIDN'T STOP TO THINK WHEN SHE SAID 'MANY HAPPY RETURNS'.

YOUR NEPHEW,
TIM

WILL,
THAT'S IT. I'M FED UP WITH THIS WORLD . . . SO I'M GOING TO KILL MYSELF. I INTEND TO JUMP OFF A TEN STORY BUILDING. SINCE WE DON'T HAVE A TEN STORY BUILDING IN TOWN I'LL HAVE TO JUMP OFF A FIVE STORY BUILDING TWICE.

G'BYE,
JACK

Priest: "Do you realize madam that in this confessional you've been telling me the same sin about you and that man for the past three years."

Woman: "Yes, Father, I knows that, but I just loves to be talking about it."

"Did you hear about old Kelly?"

"Shure, an 'twas himself that fell off a seventy-five-foot ladder."

"Oh my! Poor Kelly. He must have been terribly hurt."

"Not at all! Shure the old fool only fell off the second rung."

TIMELESS... EPITAPHS

DID YOUR MILLIONAIRE UNCLE REMEMBER YOU IN HIS WILL? HE MUST HAVE—HE NEVER MENTIONED ME.

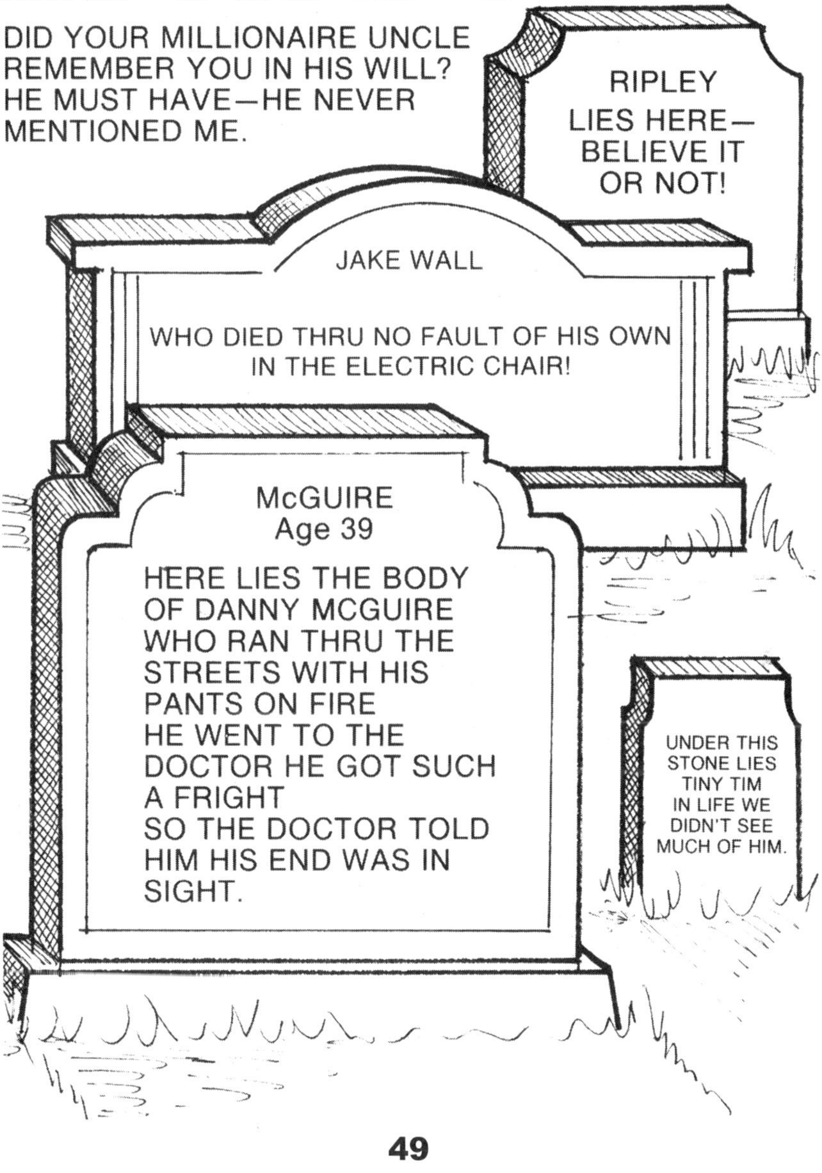

At the King's Bridge bar, he saw a simply gorgeous blond wearing the tightest pair of Levis he'd ever seen.

So, he sat next to her and when he got up his nerve said, "Sweetheart, how in heck do you ever get into those pants?"

"Well," she replied, "You can start by buying me a Manhattan."

The Mountie was cruising on highway 401 when he saw the Newfoundlander knitting – driving at the highest speed, and steering the car with his knees.

Enraged, the Mountie drove alongside and shouted. "Pullover! Pullover!"

"Nope," said the Newfoundlander, unconcerned. "It's a cardigan."

I paid a hundred dollars for that dog, part collie and part bull.

Which part was bull?

The part about the hundred dollars.

Jake: "Hey, Pete. Where did you get that shiner?"

Pete: "That happened when I kissed the bride after the ceremony."

Jake: "But isn't that the custom?"

Pete: "Yeah – But this was three years after."

The doctor told me he could fix up me face and take the redness and the swelling from me nose. The secret – I'd have to give up drinking whiskey. I was horrified.

"Wot," sez I, "all that for a nose!"

I lost me use for drinkin' water when I found out what fish did in it.

I am now working on me second million. I give up all hope of me first.

When you come right down to it, t'was me wife that started me drinkin' and I think it's only common courtesy for me to thank her.

CROSSWORD PUZZLE

ACROSS

1. A sharp blow with fist
2. Tool used to put holes in leather
3. Judy's friend
4. Type of fruit drink
5. A magazine

DOWN

1. Vegetable
2. Female sheep
3. Lays eggs
4. Oceans
5. Often dropped

1 P	2 U	3 N	4 C	5 H
2 P	U	N	C	H
3 P	U	N	C	H
4 P	U	N	C	H
5 P	U	N	C	H

NEWFIE SWING

PROBLEM SOLVED BY . . .
TORONTONIAN ENGINEERS

DUMBBELL LETTERS

JENNY,

DARLING, LET'S TAKE OUR SAVINGS AND GO TO IRELAND. WE CAN'T HELP BUT GET RICH BECAUSE I READ IN THE GAZETTE THAT HER CAPITAL IS ALWAYS DUBLIN.

YOUR EGBERT

DEAR SIR,

I REALLY DO ADMIRE YOU. I READ THAT YOU STARTED OUT ON A SHOESTRING. I MEAN, CAN YOU JUST IMAGINE ANYONE BEING ABLE TO SELL ANYBODY JUST ONE SHOESTRING!

H. SMITH

SIR,

WOULD YOUR BANK PLEASE SEND A NEW CHEQUE BOOK. I CAN'T FIND THE ONE I HAD—I GUESS I LOST IT. BUT NO NEED TO WORRY BECAUSE I HAD SIGNED EVERY LAST ONE. SO NO ONE ELSE CAN USE THEM.

THANKS, ERMA C.

DEAR SIR,

I WANTS ANOTHER REFERENCE. I CAN'T GET A JOB WHEN I SHOWS 'EM THE ONE YOU GAVE ME—'SPECIALLY THE PART THAT SAYS THAT I WAS ONE OF THE BEST MEN YOUR FIRM EVER TURNED OUT.

ED LITTLE

DUMBBELL LETTERS

DEAR JIM,

IT WAS DARN GOOD OF YOU TO SEND ME THE HUNDRED DOLLARS. I SURE WISH I COULD HAVE USED THE MONEY—BUT UNFORTUNATELY IT SAID ON THE ENVELOPE 'RETURN IN 5 DAYS'.

(OH WELL) *TED*

SIR,

IT WAS NICE OF YOUR BANK TO RETURN MY CHEQUE—NOW I CAN GO SHOPPING AND BUY SOMETHING REALLY NICE.

THANK YOU,
MABEL SMITH

WILBUR,

YOU TOLD ME THAT I WAS ONE IN A MILLION. WELL SO FAR AS I'M CONCERNED SO ARE YOUR CHANCES.

HELEN

DEAR SIR,

I WISH YOUR STUPID BANK WOULDN'T PESTER ME WITH THOSE SILLY NOTES TELLING ME I'M OVER DRAWN. HAS IT EVER OCCURRED TO YOU THAT ALL THE REST OF MY CHEQUES ARE PROBABLY NOT IN YET?

MAE WHITE

DUMBBELL LETTERS

MOTHER,

WHAT YOU HEARD ISN'T TRUE. JIM AND I DON'T FIGHT. ACTUALLY THE ONLY TIME THAT WORDS PASSED BETWEEN US WAS WHEN HE THREW A BOWL OF ALPHABET SOUP AT ME.

LOVE ETHEL

DARLING,

WE'RE BOTH AT THE AGE WHEN WE SHOULD HAVE SOME FUN. WE SHOULD GO OUT TONITE AND GET DRUNK AND HAVE A REAL SEXY NITE.

YOUR ED

P.S. IF YOU GET HOME BEFORE ME PLEASE LEAVE ON THE HALL LIGHT.

DEAR JIM,

MY WIFE IS MAD AT ME—(CAN I COME AND STAY WITH YOU?) SHE SAYS EVERY ROOM SHE GOES IN HAS ALL KINDS OF EMPTY BOTTLES. FUNNY THING IS I DON'T REMEMBER BRINGING HOME ANY EMPTY ONES.

PETE

SARA,

PLEASE STOP BEING ANGRY JUST BECAUSE YOU SAW ME COMING OUT OF A BEER PARLOUR. LOOK AT IT THIS WAY—I HAD TO COME OUT SOMETIME.

LOVE, WILLIAM

Henry: "Look oldtimer, I don't want to brag. But to give you some idea of the size of my land, two days ago I got in my car to drive around it and I didn't get here until this morning."

Farmer: "Yep, I know what you mean, young feller. I had a car like that once."

SIGNS TO GIVE YOU A CHUCKLE..

BARBER SHOP SIGNS

DUMBBELL LETTERS

"I say, conductor, will you please get me a glass of water?"

"That's the tenth glass of water I've gotten you in the last five minutes. I never heard of anyone drinking so much."

"I'm not drinking it. My berth is on fire. I'm trying to put it out."

"I wonder why this suit only has three pockets in it."

"I doubt the manufacturer knew anyone who buys a cheap suit like that wouldn't have much to put in the pockets."

The man walked into the bar and sat down on the barstool, ordered six double rums and paid for them, jumped up on the bar and walked on his hands to the far wall, walked straight up the wall and upside down, he walked across the ceiling to the entrance wall and then out the door.

Said one of the astonished customers, "Did you see that?"

"Yeah," said the bartender. "That son of a gun never tips."

REMEMBER WHEN...

There was no such thing as TV news to keep up with current events; all you had to do was visit the local barber shop.

When you were a small boy you saw a man putting a feedbag on a horse and you walked up to him and told him to give up because you knew he'd never get that horse in such a small bag.

When you wouldn't dare mention sex, read a dirty book, or even mention a couple staying overnight in a hotel room – but you thought nothing of Tarzan shacked up in a tree with Jane.

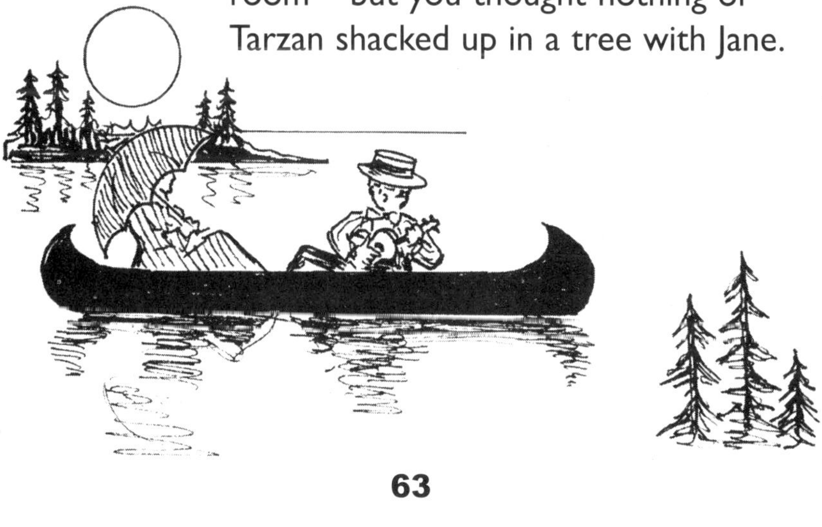

Pat: "Y'know Reilly, I've come to the conclusion that the way me mother-in-law keeps on jabberin' so much she must have been vaccinated with a gramophone needle."

The fog was very thick, so Pat was following the tail lights of the car ahead when all of a sudden the car stopped and Pat crashed into it. Putting his head out the window, Pat yelled at the other driver. "Why the hell didn't you let me know that you were going to stop?"

The other driver yelled back. "Shure, and why should I? I'm in me own garage!"

Whoever is responsible for all the violence on television ought to be mugged, stabbed, assaulted, maimed and boiled alive.

A fellow got out of his car and walked back to the old skipper and said, "My bumper is bent. What are you going to do about it?"

Angry that the car ahead had stopped with no brake lights, Skipper said,

Kiss my rear."

The fellow in the front car went back to his girlfriend. "It's okay, dear. He wants to settle out of court."

"Look baby," he said, "I'm a man of few words. Will you or won't you?"

Said the lass, "You talked me into it."

"My darling, would you be liking to have dinner with me tonight?"

"Why sure Pat, I'd love it."

"Great! I'll be over to your house at seven. Tell yer mudder not to burn the gravy."

REMEMBER WHEN.

AT THE CIRCUS A MAN
FELL OFF THE WHEEL.
EVERYBODY LAUGHED
BUT ME—
I HAPPENED TO
BE THE MAN.

IT'S A
LAUGH—A—MINUTE.

HOT DOGS
USED TO BE
A NICKEL.

REMEMBER WHEN YOU TOOK OUT A GIRL FOR A RIDE IN YOUR AUTOMOBILE AND SLYLY RAN OUT OF GAS AND WHEN YOU TOLD HER SHE'D SMILE SWEETLY AND COYLY PULLED OUT A FLASK - AND WHEN YOU'D ASK "WHAT KIND IS IT DARLING," SHE WOULD FLUTTER HER EYES AND REPLY "GASOLINE - NOW LET'S GET MOVING."

AND MURPHY WHO WANTED TO BE A LION TAMER - HE STEPPED INTO THE CAGE WITHOUT ARMS AND CAME BACK WITHOUT LEGS.

NOW I LAY ME DOWN TO SLEEP
IN MY TRUNDLE BED
IF I SHOULD DIE BEFORE I WAKE
HOW WILL THEY KNOW I'M DEAD?

SARGE—LOOK HERE, DO YOU KNOW I FOUND A BARREL OF WHISKEY IN YOUR ROOM?

RECRUIT—I KNOWS SIR—'TIS ORDERS FROM ME DOCTOR. HE TOLT ME THAT DRINKIN' WOULD RESTORE ME HEALTH.

SARGE—WELL, DID IT?

RECRUIT—WELL, SIR, WHEN I FIRST BOUGHT THAT BARREL I'D ALL I COULD DO TO MOVE IT. BUT SINCE I BEEN DRINKIN' THE WHISKEY I KIN PUSH IT ALL OVER THE PLACE.

DUMBBELL LETTERS

DEAR SIRS,

PLEASE CANCEL MY ORDER FOR A WORLD ATLAS. AFTER GIVING IT SOME THOUGHT I'VE DECIDED TO WAIT TILL WORLD AFFAIRS GET A BIT MORE SETTLED.

ANGUS MACDONALD

ANGUS,

WHEN YE COME TO NEWFOUNDLAND I'M AFRAID YE'LL FIND THE BOAT TRIP VERY ROUGH. I'VE FOUND THAT FER US THE ONE SURE WAY TO PREVENT SEA SICKNESS IS TO PUT A QUARTER BETWEEN YER TEETH.

REGARDS, *SCOTTY*

DARLING,

ST. JOHN'S HAS TO BE THE RUDEST TOWN I'VE EVER BEEN IN. WHY, DO YOU KNOW, I'VE BEEN ASKIN' PEOPLE THE TIME ALL DAY—AND EVERY SINGLE TIME THEY GIVE ME A DIFFERENT ANSWER.

(FED UP) *MARTHA*

WHAT TIME IS IT SPIKE?
HOW'D Y'KNOW ME NAME IS SPIKE?
I GUESSED IT.
WELL, GUESS THE BLOODY TIME THEN.

WENT INTO O'TOOLE'S BOOK STORE ON WATER STREET, FEELING DEPRESSED . . . SAW A BOOK TITLED "HOW TO BE HAPPY WITHOUT MONEY". I BOUGHT IT. (THE BOOK COST $40.00.)

I HAPPENS T'HAVE THE WORST MOTHER-IN-LAW IN TOWN. SHE WAS DRUMMED OUT OF THE GESTAPO FOR CRUELTY.

How is Murphy?

He's lying at death's door.
That's grit for you—at death's door an' still lying.

KIN YE' BELIEVE THIS. . . .

I TOLT ME SON T' WASH HIS HANDS AN' HE SAYS "WOT, BOTH OF 'EM?"
SO I SEZ . . . "NAW JEST ONE. WANTS T' SEE HOW YOU DOES IT." (HEH, HEH)

During the war they wanted me to join a submarine crew. "Not me, I sez. I'm not gettin' on any ship that sinks on purpose!"

Accountant: When you called up my wife and told her I would be detained at the office, and would not be home until very late, what did she say:

Boss: Can I depend on that?

"How long have you been working here?" asked the boss.

So I tolt him. "Ever since I seen you coming up the steps."

TWO OF US REPORTERS WERE SENT TO CHECK ON A LIVE WIRE THAT FELL ACROSS WATER STREET. ONE OF US TO TOUCH THE WIRE; AND THE OTHER TO WRITE THE STORY.

Teacher: "Never in my whole life have I seen such a dirty hand. Johnny, you're going to get well caned for that. If you can show me another hand anywhere in the school that is dirtier, then I'll let you off."

"So long." Johnny held out his other hand.

"Bill's lost his coat again."

"How's that?"

"Can't find mine."

"How's your uncle doing with his farm?"

"Not so good. There ain't much money in milk and eggs anymore. So he sits up all night trying to think of something else for the hens and cows to do."

FROM THE PAGES OF . . .

JAKE, THE WIFE SAID TO ME, "I'M A WOMAN OF FEW WORDS AND IF I BECKON WITH MY FINGER THAT MEANS COME, AND COME QUICKLY."

AND I SAID TO HER, "I'M A MAN OF FEW WORDS MYSELF AND IF I SHAKE MY HEAD THAT MEANS I AIN'T COMING."

SO YOUR BROTHER-IN-LAW LOST HIS JOB AS A BUTLER, JIGGER.
YEAH, THEY TOLD HIM TO CALL THE NAMES OF ALL THE GUESTS AS THEY ARRIVED AT THE PARTY.
WELL, COULDN'T HE DO THAT?
YEAH, BUT SOME OF THE NAMES HE CALLED THEM CAN'T BE REPEATED.

JAKE, HERE'S AN OLD NEWFOUNDLAND SAYING...

I JUST MADE THIS UP:
NO MAN GOES BEFORE HIS TIME, UNLESS OF COURSE THE BOSS LEAVES EARLY.

JAKE, IT WAS ON WALL STREET THAT I LOST EVERY CENT I HAD.
IS THAT THE TRUTH, JIGGER?
YEAH, I WAS STANDING ON THIS VERY CORNER WHEN I STUMBLED AND FELL, DROPPING MY LAST LOONEY IN THE SEWER.

JIGGER, CAN YOU CHANGE A DOLLAR FOR ME?
ALMOST, JAKE.
I CAN CHANGE SIXTY-FIVE CENTS FOR IT.

JAKE, I SAW SIX PEOPLE STANDING UNDER AN UMBRELLA AND NOT ONE OF THEM GOT WET.
HOW COME NOBODY GOT WET, JIGGER?
'CAUSE IT WASN'T RAINING, I GUESS.

I GOT RID OF THE NOISE IN THE REAR WHEN I DROVE A TAXI, JAKE.
HOW DID YA DO IT, JIGGER?
I MADE HER SIT UP FRONT WITH ME.

JAKE, GUESS WHAT? WE GOT A NEW BABY AT OUR HOUSE AND EVERYONE IS SOME EXCITED.
WHY, JIGGER, DID YOU TURN IN THE OLD ONE?

MY SISTER'S NEW BABY IS JUST TWO AND A HALF WEEKS OLD AND SHE'S COMING OVER TO OUR HOUSE.
WHAT'S ITS NAME, JIGGER?
I DUNNO, BOY. I CAN'T UNDERSTAND A WORD IT SAYS.

THE BOSS SAID WHEN HE HIRED ME IF I DID MY WORK WELL WE WOULD TALK ABOUT A RAISE.
AH WELL JAKE, I MIGHT HAVE KNOWN THERE'D BE A CATCH TO IT.

Y'KNOW JAKE, I ONCE HAD A JOB ASSEMBLING IN A PARACHUTING FACTORY.
DID YOU HAVE ANY PROBLEMS, JIGGER?
NO ONE HAS COMPLAINED OF A PARACHUTE NOT OPENING.

ME UNCLE WILL WAS BEFORE COURT, BUT WHEN THEY TRIED HIM THE JUDGE LET HIM GO FREE.
THAT RIGHT, JIGGER?
YEAH, UNCLE WILL WAS DEAF AN' AS ANYONE KIN TELL YOU, YOU CAN'T CONVICT A MAN WITHOUT A HEARING.

WHERE DID YOUR COUSIN MEET HIS GIRL, JIGGER?

BELIEVE IT OR NOT, JAKE, HE MET HER IN A REVOLVING DOOR AND HE'S BEEN GOING AROUND WITH HER EVER SINCE.

I'M NOT AS STINGY AS MY UNCLE – ONE DAY HE WAS WALKING THROUGH THE ALLEY AND HE FOUND ON THE GROUND A PACKAGE FILLED TO THE BRIM WITH UNTOUCHED COUGH-DROPS.

SO WHAT DID HE DO, JIGGER?

THAT NIGHT HE MADE HIS WIFE SLEEP OUT IN THE GARDEN SO THAT SHE WOULD CATCH A COLD.

JAKE, ON THINKING IT OVER, I MADE MY DECISION TO REFUSE THE OFFER AS THE PRESIDENT OF A BUSINESS COMPANY.
WHY DID YOU DO THAT, JIGGER?
BECAUSE THERE WAS NO CHANCE FOR ADVANCEMENT.

JIGGER, HOW DID YOU GET THAT BLACK EYE?

WELL JAKE, YOU KNOW
THAT BEAUTIFUL BLOND
WHOSE HUSBAND IS IN
CHINA?

WELL, HE ISN'T IN CHINA.

JAKE, I TOLD MAGGIE, "I'M GOING TO KISS YOU TONIGHT OR DIE IN THE ATTEMPT."
WELL JIGGER, DID YOU?
YOU DIDN'T SEE MY NAME IN THE OBITUARY COLUMN, DID YOU?

JAKE, THE JUDGE ASKED ME, "YOUNG FELLOW, HAVE YOU EVER BEEN UP BEFORE ME?"

AND I SAID, "I DON'T KNOW, YER HONOUR, WHAT TIME DO YOU GET UP?

JIGGER, I'D LIKE TO KNOW IF I HAVE GROUNDS FOR A DIVORCE.
ARE YOU MARRIED, JAKE?
YES.
THEN OF COURSE YOU HAVE.

HE WAS TO GET A MEDAL FOR BRAVERY BUT THEY COULDN'T GIVE IT TO HIM, JAKE.
WHY NOT, JIGGER?
HE WAS SO UGLY THEY COULDN'T FIND A FRENCH GENERAL WHO WOULD KISS HIM.

I HEAR YOU TOOK THAT CHORUS GIRL OUT TO DINNER. WHAT DID SHE HAVE?
SOUP, SALAD, FISH, CHICKEN, DESSERT AND COFFEE.
WHAT DID YOU HAVE?
HEART FAILURE.

JIGGER, I JUST GOT A
NOTICE FROM THE BANK
SAYING I'M OVERDRAWN.

TRY SOME OTHER
BANK, JAKE. THEY
CAN'T ALL BE
OVERDRAWN.

WHAT CAN I DO
FOR YOU, JIGGER?
I WANT A HAT.
FEDORA?
NO, FOR ME.

WHEN I FIRST WENT TO NEW YORK I HAD ONLY A DOLLAR IN MY POCKET WITH WHICH TO MAKE A START.
JIGGER, HOW DID YOU INVEST THAT DOLLAR?
USED IT TO PAY FOR A TELEGRAM HOME FOR MORE MONEY.

I CAME IN HERE TO GET SOMETIHNG FOR MY WIFE, JIGGER.
WHAT ARE YOU ASKING FOR HER?

I ONCE STOLE MONEY, JAKE.

WHERE DID YOU STEAL IT FROM, JIGGER?

A BANK.

HOW MUCH DID YOU STEAL?

A HALF DOLLAR.

WHAT BANK WAS IT?

MY BABY SON'S.

JAKE, I ASKED THE JUDGE, “WHAT FLOOR IS THIS, YOUR HONOUR?” “THE FIFTH FLOOR,” HE SAID. “IN THAT CASE, I’M GOING UPSTAIRS.”
WHAT FOR?
I SAID, “I WANT TO BE TRIED IN A HIGHER COURT.”

THE JUDGE SAID,
"HAVE YOU A LAWYER?"

"NO," I SAID, "BUT I HAVE SOME
GOOD FRIENDS ON THE JURY."

JIGGER, WHAT ARE YOU GOING TO GIVE ME FOR CHRISTMAS?
CLOSE YOUR EYES AND TELL ME WHAT YOU SEE.
NOTHING.
THAT'S WHAT YOU'RE GOING TO GET FOR CHRISTMAS.

JAKE, THAT MOUTH ORGAN YOU GAVE ME FOR MY BIRTHDAY IS EASILY THE BEST PRESENT I'VE HAD.
I'M GLAD YOU LIKE IT.
YES – MOTHER GIVES ME A QUARTER A WEEK NOT TO PLAY IT.

YA KNOW, JAKE, THERE'S NEVER BEEN A BIG MAN BORN IN ST. JOHN'S.
THAT RIGHT, JIGGER?
YEAH, ALL WE GETS ARE BABIES.

SEE THESE STOCKINGS, JAKE? I JUST PAID FIVE DOLLARS FOR THEM. THEY'RE A GIFT FOR MY GIRL. DO YOU THINK SHE'LL LIKE THEM?
WHY, THERE'S A RUN IN EACH STOCKING.
YEAH – I DID THAT – I WANTED TO GET A RUN FOR MY MONEY.

YESTERDAY WHILE WE WERE OUT HUNTING YOU ALMOST SHOT MY MOTHER-IN-LAW, JIGGER

SORRY, HERE'S MY GUN. TAKE A SHOT AT MINE.

HOW DID HE DIE?

HE PASSED AWAY DURING A CARD GAME.

WHAT DID HE DIE OF?

FIVE ACES.

WELL JAKE, SOMETHING
TERRIBLE HAS HAPPENED TO ME.

I WAS WALKING ALONG WITH MY
FRIEND DAVID AND HE SAID,
"SOMEBODY IS FOLLOWING US."

"WHO IS IT?" I ASKED. DAVID SAID,
"I DON'T KNOW," AND THEN A MAN
CAME UP AND HANDED ME THIS
BIG PIECE OF PAPER."

NO, HE WAS
AFTER ME.

JAKE, I ASKED MY GIRL'S FATHER WOULD HE CONSENT TO ME MARRYING HIS DAUGHTER AND HE REPLIED, "I DUNNO, CAN YOU SUPPORT A FAMILY?"
WHAT DID YOU SAY, JIGGER?
SO I SAID TO HIM, "I GUESS SO – HOW MANY OF YOU ARE THERE?"

JAKE, THEY SAY OUR PREMIER
IS A FELLER WOT TAKES HIS
HAT OFF TO NOBODY...

THAT RIGHT,
JIGGER?

WONDER HOW HE GETS
HIS HAIR CUT?

YA KNOW JAKE, ME AN' NELL
HAVE BEEN MARRIED 10 YEARS
AN' ME MOTHER-IN-LAW HAS
ONLY VISITED US ONCE.

THAT RIGHT,
JIGGER?

YEP, SHE CAME THE DAY
AFTER WE WERE MARRIED
AN' NEVER LEFT!

Y'KNOW JAKE, WE WERE
NEVER WHAT Y'CALL
WELL-OFF.

THAT RIGHT,
JIGGER?

WHEN I WAS OLD ENOUGH TO BUY ME OWN CLOTHES I WALKED FROM ONE END OF WATER STREET TO THE OTHER LOOKIN' FOR SHORTS WITH "ROBIN HOOD FLOUR" PRINTED ON THEM.

JAKE, ME NEW EMPLOYER TOLD ME THAT MY SALARY IS PERSONAL AND NOT TO BE DISCLOSED TO ANYONE.

"DON'T WORRY ABOUT IT," I TOLD HIM, "I'M JUST AS ASHAMED OF IT AS YOU."

I KNOWS WHAT POOR IS...
THAT RIGHT, JIGGER?
Y'KNOW JAKE, I WAS TWELVE YEARS OLD BEFORE I KNEW A TURKEY HAD ANY MORE THAN A NECK.

AH JAKE, I REMEMBERS WHEN IT WAS SO COLD IN OUR HOUSE OUR NEXT DOOR NEIGHBOUR USED TO ASK MUDDER IF SHE COULD PUT HER JELLY IN MY ROOM!

JAKE, YOU MIGHT NOT THINK OF ME AS HANDSOME, BUT EVERY DAY I'M ASKED TO GET MARRIED.
BY WHO, JIGGER?
ME MOTHER AND FATHER.

AH JAKE, SOME PEOPLE HAVE THE GIFT FOR MAKING MONEY – EVERYTHING ME BRUDDER TOUCHES TURNS TO GOLD.
THAT RIGHT, JIGGER?
NOT ME THOUGH – EVERYTHING I TOUCHES THEY MAKES ME PUT BACK.

JAKE, THE NEXT WOMAN I MARRY
WILL BE A WOMAN WHO CAN SEW...

Y'KNOW, THE KIND YOU CAN GIVE A HANDFUL
OF BUTTONS AN' SAY HERE, SEW SOME SHIRTS
ON THESE.

Y'KNOW JAKE, ONLY ONCE DID ANY HOT WORDS PASS BETWEEN ME AN' THE MISSUS.

THAT RIGHT, JIGGER?

YEP, T'WAR WHEN SHE THREW A POT OF ALPHABET SOUP AT ME.

JAKE, ME WIFE SAYS SHE DIDN'T HAVE A RAG ON HER BACK WHEN SHE MARRIED ME.
THAT RIGHT, JIGGER?
WELL, SHE GOT PLENTY OF THEM NOW.

JAKE, YOU ASKED ME IF I CAME FROM NEWFOUNDLAND. AS LONG AS YOU WANT TO KNOW – YES I DID.
WHAT PART, JIGGER?
ALL OF ME!

JAKE, I TOLD MY WIFE THAT
WE SHOULD HAVE SOME FUN
THIS EVENING.

SHE SAID, "THAT'S GREAT HONEY, I'VE WANTED TO DO THAT FOR A LONG TIME – I'LL REALLY ENJOY IT, AND IF YOU GET HOME BEFORE ME, BE A DEAR AND LEAVE THE LIGHT ON IN THE HALL."

JAKE, TODAY I SAT DOWN AND WROTE MY DEAR WIFE A VERY LONG, LOVING LETTER.

BUT JIGGER, YOU KNOW YOU CAN'T WRITE.

WHAT'S THE DIFFERENCE? SHE CAN'T READ!

JAKE, I NEED TO GET ONE HUNDRED AND SIXTY SQUARE HOLES BY TUESDAY.

I NEEDS TO GET THEM FOR THIS WEEK I PROMISED TO MAKE A FISH NET.

JAKE, MY WIFE AND MYSELF HAD A ROW TODAY BECAUSE OF ME EATING WITH ME FINGERS

BUT I TOLD HER – IF THE FOOD WASN'T CLEAN ENOUGH TO PICK UP WITH MY FINGERS THEN IT WASN'T FIT TO EAT.

AH JAKE, WORK, WORK ALL DAY LONG, FROM MORN UNTIL LATE AT NIGHT.

HOW LONG HAVE YOU BEEN IN THAT JOB, JIGGER?

WHO, ME? I STARTS TOMORROW.

THE JUDGE ASKED ME UNCLE IF HE HAD ANYTHING TO OFFER THE COURT BEFORE HE WAS TO BE SENTENCED.

AND WHAT DID YOUR UNCLE SAY, JIGGER?

HE SAID, "NO YOUR HONOUR, MY LAWYER TOOK MY LAST DOLLAR."

JAKE, MY WIFE IS COOKING AN
ENTHUSIASTIC STEW FOR SUPPER.

I CALLS IT ENTHUSIASTIC STEW BECAUSE SHE
PUTS EVERYTHING INTO IT.

JAKE, WHEN THE DAY IS FINISHED I REFUSE TO TAKE MY TROUBLES TO BED.

YES B'Y, YOU SEE MY WIFE WON'T SLEEP BY HERSELF.

JAKE, QUIT CALLING ME A HENPECKED NEWFIE SHRIMP – BY JAPERS YOU WOULDN'T CALL ME THAT IF MY MISSUS WERE HERE NOW.

Y'KNOW JAKE, I'VE FINALLY TAKEN THE TIME TO WRITE MYSELF A SERIOUS LETTER.

THAT'S FINE JIGGER, WHAT DOES IT SAY?

HOW THE HECK DO I KNOW? I WON'T GET IT UNTIL TUESDAY!

Y'KNOW JAKE, I DON'T KNOW WHO I AM – I WAS LEFT ON THE NUN'S DOORSTEP WHEN I WAS A LITTLE BABY.

THAT RIGHT, JIGGER?

I WONDER IF I'M A BOTTLE OF MILK?

JAKE, MY SON WANTED ME TO MEET HIM AT THE AIRPORT.
WELL, DID YOU?
AHH, NO B'Y. SURE I'VE KNOWN HIM ALL ME LIFE.

AH JAKE, THINGS ARE SOME BAD
HERE IN CANADA – OH MY, OH MY.

HOW COME,
JIGGER?

SURE I WENT BANKRUPT THREE TIMES AND
DIDN'T MAKE A DIME EITHER TIME.

I'M NOT UP ON WOMEN'S FASHIONS. MY WIFE ASKED ME IF I WOULD LIKE TO SEE HER IN SOMETHING LONG AND FLOWING.

WHAT DID YOU TELL HER, JIGGER?

I SAID, "GO JUMP IN RENNIES RIVER."

JAKE, I'M NOT WORKING HERE ANYMORE BECAUSE ME AND THE BOSS HAD A DISAGREE-MENT AND HE WON'T TAKE BACK WHAT HE SAID.
WHAT DID HE SAY, JIGGER?
YOU'RE FIRED!

JAKE, I HAD A GOOD SITUATION –
EASY WORK AND GOOD PAY.

I GAVE IT UP DUE TO ILLNESS – THE
BOSS IN CHARGE OF THE SHIFT
WORKERS GOT SICK OF ME.

JAKE, I ONCE HAD A DANDY WATCH. THREE YEARS AGO I DROPPED IT IN RENNIES RIVER. THEN ONE DAY I FOUND IT AND IT'S STILL RUNNING TO THIS DAY.
THE SAME WATCH?
NO, RENNIES RIVER.

AND NOW WE'LL HAVE A SNAKE DANCE – GIVING ALL THOSE WHO SNAKED IN WITHOUT PAYING THE CHANCE TO SNAKE OUT AGAIN.

JAKE, THE JUDGE THAT HEARD MY CASE WAS NOT ONLY STUPID, BUT YOU COULD TELL THAT HE WAS BLIND.

THREE TIMES HE ASKED, "WHERE'S MY HAT?" AND THE WHOLE TIME IT WAS ON MY HEAD.

JAKE, I REALLY NEED TO SEE A DOCTOR. I CAN'T EVEN REMEMBER WHAT HAPPENED YESTERDAY!

HOW LONG HAVE YOU HAD THIS PROBLEM, JIGGER?

WHAT PROBLEM?

JIGGER, HOW COME YOU REALLY HAVE
NO TIME FOR PETE?

WELL JAKE, I DON'T LIKE HIM AT ALL. IF YOU WERE DROWNING, HE'S THE KIND OF FELLOW WHO WOULD THROW YOU BOTH ENDS OF THE ROPE.

JAKE, THE JUDGE ASKED ME IF I WANTED TO CHALLENGE ANY MEMBER OF THE JURY.

SO I TOLD HIM, “YOUR HONOUR, I THINK I COULD LICK THAT LITTLE OLD MAN WITH THE BALD HEAD.

Y'KNOW JAKE, I FINALLY FIGURED OUT THE REASON THAT I'M SO DEPRESSED...I'M HOMESICK.
BUT JIGGER, THIS IS YOUR HOME.
EXACTLY, I'M SICK OF IT.

TOO BAD ABOUT O'TOOLE. I THOUGHT HIS BUSINESS WAS BOOMING. HE MUST HAVE FAILED AND IS NOW ON WELFARE.

I JUST SAW HIM DRIVING A CADILLAC.

About the Author

The late Derm Duggan was an interior designer, ventriloquist, inventor, drummer in a swing band, signmaker, and funnyman who has illustrated twenty books. His first love was painting.

Other fine books published by Flanker Press

New Release for 2009

Allan Square is a dark yet humorous coming-of-age story about a young girl growing up during the 1940s and 1950s in one of the roughest neighbourhoods in St. John's. Shirley Murphy was only seven years old when her father died and life as she knew it changed forever. Poor and often hungry, she lived with an alcoholic stepfather, a combative mother, and four brothers who treated her the way only brothers can. In *Allan Square*, Shirley vividly describes attending wakes at the homes of the deceased (for the food), trading kisses with ushers for admission to the Capitol Theatre, soaking up the sights and sounds of Water Street, and surviving a dysfunctional family in the St. John's urban playground of Livingstone Street, Allan Square, Theatre Hill, and Queen's Road.

From adventures in a school run by strict and unforgiving nuns, to heated battles with an angry mother, to nightly Acts of Contrition, this memoir is Shirley Murphy's laugh-out-loud tale of childhood antics and misspent youth in Newfoundland and Labrador's capital city.

Other fine books published by Flanker Press

"J. A. Ricketts's *The Badger Riot* is a rare combination for a historical novel: It is gripping and accurate. It is historical fiction done right."

Globe and Mail

THE NUMBER ONE SELLING BOOK
IN ATLANTIC CANADA FOR 2008.

In 1959, the small town of Badger was the centre of a labour confrontation that forever changed the social and political landscape of Newfoundland. For two and a half months, loggers had been striking for better wages and working conditions. Led by the International Woodworkers of America (IWA), the strike reached its climax when national and provincial police forces stormed the town in an attempt to break the impasse. *The Badger Riot* tells the story of the deadly melee that followed. This work of fiction captures for the first time the horror of a small community of people still reeling in shock from a tragedy that could have been prevented.

Other fine books published by Flanker Press

"*Ryan's Commander: The Boat That Should Not Have Sailed* (Flanker Press) is a book that you simply can't put down."

The Newfoundland Herald

The *Ryan's Commander* capsized off Spillars Cove, near Bonavista, on September 19, 2004. In the tragic wreck, two brothers were lost: Dave and Joe "June" Ryan. A federal report concluded that vessel design was one of the factors causing the capsizing. The family of the Ryan brothers recently filed suit against the federal government and the makers of the vessel, arguing its design was unsafe and untrustworthy. This book is Johanna Ryan Guy's tribute, both to her brothers and to the family that still mourns their loss.

Other fine books published by Flanker Press

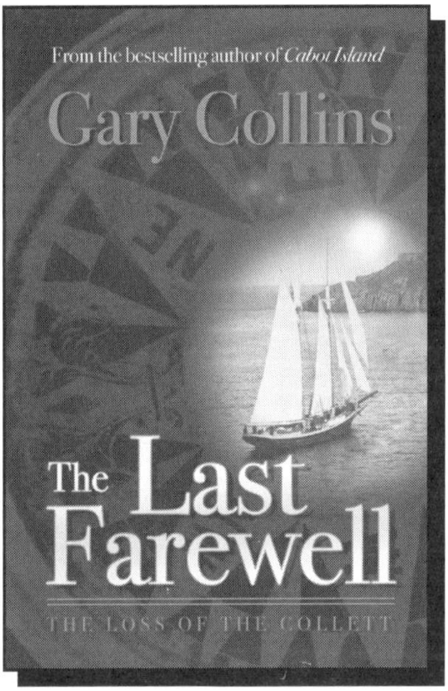

"*The Last Farewell* tells a true story, but Collins's vivid description and well-realized characters make it read like a novel."
The Chronicle Herald

INSPIRED BY TRUE EVENTS

The Last Farewell tells the true story of a crew of logger-sailors who left their home port of Hare Bay aboard a two-masted schooner in early June of 1934. Along her route to St. John's, the crew of the *Ethel Collett* tell each other stories of life and death on the sea. They relive some of Newfoundland's richest historical moments, from shipwrecks and sealing disasters to political strife and financial ruin. But little do they know that they are heading toward one of the most astonishing tales of them all: their own.

Other fine books published by Flanker Press

"Collins's focus on an ordinary event taking place under extraordinary circumstances sheds a tender, respectful light on how strength of character can be forged at the anguished intersection of isolation and bereavement."

Downhome

In November of 1954, a terrible storm darkened the skies above Cabot Island and battered its solitary lighthouse with a single-minded fury. The keepers of the Cabot Island light were no strangers to sea weather, but when tragedy struck the brothers Gill, the younger of the two was left to fend for himself amid one of the worst storms in Newfoundland's history. This is a true story of the love between two brothers, a love that perseveres in the face of death, loss, and greatest personal challenge.